Bank Consolidation and Small Business Lending: The Role of Community Banks

Bank Consolidation and Small Business Lending:
The Role of Community Banks

This paper examines how bank merger and acquisition activity affected small business lending in local U.S. banking markets between 1994 and 2000, focusing particularly on the role that community banks played in determining the ultimate effects of consolidation. During the 1994–1997 period, we find evidence that consolidation activity involving big banks was associated with lower loan growth, whereas community bank consolidations and a greater presence of community banks in the market were associated with higher loan growth. During the 1997–2000 period, consolidation activity was either unrelated to small business loan growth or associated with higher loan growth, suggesting that the dynamics of consolidation activity had changed. In both periods, we find evidence that consolidation presented an opportunity for community banks. Once adjustments are made for reclassifications in the size category of organizations due to consolidation or asset growth, we find that the share of small business lending funded by community banks rose during both study periods—particularly in markets undergoing consolidation.

The U.S. banking industry has undergone a substantial consolidation over the past decade, raising questions about the viability of the traditional community bank. Concerns have been raised that community banks may not be able to compete effectively against larger organizations enjoying the benefits of scale economies in product offerings and cost savings. On the other hand, consolidation may also offer opportunities for community banks to take on business abandoned by large consolidating organizations. Small business lending is thought to be the area in which community banks are most likely to have these niche opportunities because such lending is both less likely to evidence economies of scale and more likely to benefit from a local presence.

In this paper we provide evidence addressing the appropriateness of these concerns. We study how consolidation activity has been related to changes in small business lending in local banking markets and examine whether the presence of community banks in a market can be a mitigating factor in offsetting contractions in small business lending that might otherwise take place as a result of consolidation. Although the question of the survival of community banks is of interest to those concerned about industry structure, the potential loss of valuable products and services is the more important social issue. If community banks can be shown to provide services and products that would otherwise be lost in consolidation, efforts to ensure their survival would be socially appropriate.

The link between community banking and small business lending has long been recognized. Traditionally, this type of lending has been local in nature—often to firms having idiosyncratic credit needs and risks tied to the prospects of the local economy. Thus, small business lending has generally required the local expertise that personifies the community bank in terms of underwriting and monitoring firm-specific risks. Indeed, smaller business borrowers can find it difficult to obtain credit from lenders that do not have a local presence. This is less the case for other bank borrowers. Large commercial borrowers deal with large banks that operate in numerous markets and often syndicate loans to share the risks. Even lending to households in the form of consumer credit or home mortgages has evolved into increasingly standardized products transacted in what have become national markets. These types of loans require product-specific expertise, but they do not require the same sort of local presence as lending to small businesses.

The extent to which small business lending suits the inherently more local focus of community banks is borne out in general trends evident from 1994 through 2000 (see table 1). Community banks continue to hold a disproportionately large share of small business loans, compared with their share of total banking-industry assets.[1] However, the community bank share of small business loans has been declining—particularly the share of small business loans under $100,000 (although, as we argue below, these figures are deceptive). Consolidation is also evident during the 1994–2000 period. From mid-1994 through mid-2000, 2,870 of an original 10,341 banking organizations were consolidated through unaffiliated mergers and acquisitions, 41 were liquidated, and 864 new institutions were formed. Much of the consolidation of this period was driven by the relaxation of geographic banking restrictions, as banks sought to extend their geographic scope to other states and regions. By mid-2000, over 30 percent of banking institution deposits were in offices located in states other than where the organization was headquartered, a percentage that had more than doubled since 1991.

---

[1] Here and throughout this paper, we define community banks as independent commercial banks or savings institutions or bank or thrift holding companies that control less than $1 billion in assets (in 2000 dollars).

The traditional comparative advantage of community banks as small business lenders suggests that what happens in this product area will be critical in determining the impact of bank consolidation on the future of community banking. It also suggests that the presence (or potential for entry) of community banks may play an important role in determining the impact of consolidation on small business lending. Although a fair amount of research has addressed the impact of consolidation on banking institutions, little of it has focused specifically on community banks. Furthermore, there is almost no research that has looked at the question at a market level. Much of the reason for this omission is probably limitations in data. Balance-sheet data on a bank's outstanding small business loans (business loans of less than $1 million at origination) have been reported by commercial banks and thrifts since 1993. However, geographic data on small business loan originations are reported only by the largest banking institutions, and only since 1996.[2] These limitations represent significant hurdles to constructing reliable market-level estimates of small business lending.

In this study, we examine the relationships between the amount and types of consolidation activity in local banking markets and changes in inflation-adjusted small business lending between 1994 and 2000.[3] We deal with the limitations of balance-sheet small business loan data by using deposit data reported by banking institutions to impute the geographic distribution of each institution's small business lending. We use these geographic loan estimates to examine three interrelated questions: (1) How *local consolidation activity* (referring to

---

[2] Samolyk and Richardson (2003) discuss issues involved in using these data, which are collected under the auspices of the Community Reinvestment Act (CRA).

[3] Although the data on small business loans are available for 1993, we choose not to use these early data because of concerns about reporting problems associated with them.

acquisitions of previously unaffiliated banking institutions or holding companies by other independent banks or holding companies) is related to market-level changes in small business lending, (2) how the presence of community banks affects the impact of consolidation activity on local small business loan markets, and finally (3) how consolidation has affected community banks' role as small business lenders. To better understand the dynamics of observed relationships, we study overall changes in small business lending as well as its decomposition into loan subproducts, as illustrated in table 1. Because of inherent differences in the characteristics and economic environments of urban and rural markets, we conduct separate analyses of them for two different study periods: 1994–1997 and 1997–2000.

By way of preview, in the 1994–1997 study period we find mixed evidence on the relationship between bank consolidation and small business lending, with the outcome depending critically on the role of community banks. Consolidations involving big banking organizations are associated with lower real small business loan growth, whereas consolidations involving only community banks are associated with higher loan growth. Furthermore, in markets where community banks have a large ex ante market share, we find that the negative effects of consolidation activity are mitigated. The 1997–2000 study period reveals quite different patterns. In urban markets, consolidation activity involving big banking organizations is associated with higher small business loan growth primarily in loans of less than $100,000 and in commercial and industrial (C&I) lending. In rural markets, we also find positive effects of big bank consolidation activity, but in a different product area—commercial real estate (CRE) lending. In both urban and rural markets, we find little evidence that the degree of community bank presence influenced the impact of consolidation on small business lending during the 1997–2000 study period.

In both study periods, our analysis indicates that consolidation presented an opportunity for community banks. Uniformly, once adjustments are made for economic factors and for reclassifications in the size category of organizations due to consolidation or asset growth, we find that the small business loan market share of community banks increased. Further, the increases in market share tended to be greater in markets undergoing consolidation. These patterns are evident for total small business lending as well as for the various small business loan subproducts that we study.

The remainder of this article is organized as follows: The next section outlines the conjectures about how bank consolidation affects small business lending, summarizes the evidence regarding these conjectures, and relates this evidence to our study. Section 2 describes the methodology and the data used for our analysis. Section 3 presents our statistical tests and test results. Section 4 reports estimates that decompose small business loan growth and changes in community bank small business loan market shares into consolidation-related changes and offsetting effects by other firms in the market. Section 5 presents a discussion of robustness issues and section 6 concludes.

1. RELATED LITERATURE

The goals of this paper are to quantify the relationship between bank consolidation and small business lending at the market level and to determine whether the presence of community banks influences the relationship. In this section we review evidence and conjectures from the literature regarding these questions. Because much of the existing literature has focused on evidence at the bank level, we pay particular attention to the few studies that have conducted market-level analyses. We also emphasize evidence on the role of bank size in determining the impact of consolidation.

One argument advanced in the literature is that since the commercial loans made by smaller banks tend to be smaller and more local (because of legal loan limits or the need to diversify across borrowers), smaller institutions are more likely to develop an expertise as small business "relationship lenders." Larger banks are viewed as inherently better suited to operating in a more standardized fashion, incurring higher fixed costs that can be spread out over a broader customer base. Therefore, as banks get larger and more organizationally complex, their focus shifts to larger commercial credits or more standardized types of loan products (Berger and Udell, 1998). This view implies that as banking institutions merge into larger organizations, they are likely to reduce the share of their portfolio that funds "relationship-intensive" small business loans.

It has been argued that larger banks are likely to be more efficient lenders, not only because their scale may allow them to lower certain costs but also because they can better diversify their portfolios and therefore expand their lending to all customers, including small businesses (Strahan and Weston, 1998; Morgan and Samolyk, 2003). Hence, as institutions become larger, they may be able to make more loans in general, including more small business loans.

Evidence from studies of bank efficiency and mergers suggests that benefits from increased scale are likely to be a feature only of mergers among relatively small institutions—community banks as we have defined them here. And although larger banks may be better able to use new small business lending technologies (such as credit scoring models) than their smaller counterparts, small business loans that are too large or too information intensive (such as collateralized loans) have not proven to be well suited to credit scoring methods. Thus, because consolidation can change the size distribution of banks within a market, it can impact specific small business loan products in different ways depending on whether the loans tend to be made by institutions of a particular size.

Peek and Rosengren (1998) also argue that a bank's credit culture is a key determinant of its commercial lending activities. If small business lending is an important product line (or a desired product line) for acquiring institutions, they may increase the small business loan focus of their acquisitions over the longer term. When it is not an important product line, acquirers are likely to cut back on their acquisitions' small business lending. The difficulty in testing this conjecture is that it is not always easy to determine how small business lending fits into the culture of acquiring banks, although community banks as a class are more likely to favor such lending.

These arguments suggest that the relationship between bank consolidation and small business lending is complex and depends on many factors. A significant amount of empirical work has tried to quantify the overall relationship and to determine the importance of control factors. Because of data limitations, virtually all of these studies have focused on the lending behavior of individual banks (or banking organizations). Bank-level analyses have typically involved tests for systematic differences between the small business loan-to-asset ratios of banks involved in consolidations and those of a control group of banks that have not merged.[4] Researchers have used this approach to study different types of consolidations, such as mergers

---

[4] See Berger, Demsetz, and Strahan (1999), Berger and Udell (1998), and Samolyk (1997) for discussions of these studies.

of institutions that vary in size or that are headquartered in different states. The general picture that emerges from these studies is that mergers among smaller institutions and/or banks having more of a small business focus tend to be associated with more small businesses lending (as a proportion of the bank's assets), whereas consolidation involving larger banks tends to be associated with less. But the focus of bank-level studies on balance-sheet *ratios* makes it difficult to determine the effect of bank consolidation on the *level* of lending (measured in terms of loan dollars).

As stated above, this paper focuses on assessing the relationship between consolidation and small business lending at the *market* level. Anecdotal evidence suggests that local market conditions should matter. It has been argued that since small business lending is the most localized banking product, it should be particularly sensitive to market structure (Cyrnak, 1998). According to standard structure and performance theory, consolidation activity in highly concentrated markets is likely to have a greater effect on lending than consolidation in highly competitive markets. Consequently, the same merger may have different impacts in the various markets it affects. In markets where both the acquirer and the acquired institution operate branches before the merger (within-market mergers), the merger may lead to a reduction in lending as the market becomes less competitive and the merged institution eliminates overlap. However, the same merger may have no impact in markets where there is no ex ante overlap. Even here, some researchers have argued that out-of-market acquirers may not have the same informational advantage or interest in the local market as institutions that have a local presence (Whalen, 1995; Keeton, 1997).

Some bank-level studies have recognized the potential importance of market-level factors and have attempted to include them in their empirical analyses. These studies recognize that the behavior of other market participants is an important consideration, since it can potentially offset

any adverse effects of bank consolidation on small business credit availability. Research on

other bank products suggests that the reaction of other local lenders is a critical component of the

overall impact of consolidation on the market and that failure to consider it may lead to

erroneous conclusions.[5] Two recent studies have tried to incorporate these considerations into

their analyses of consolidation and small business lending. Berger et al. (1998) use proprietary

micro loan-level data from the Federal Reserve Board of Governors Survey of the Terms of Bank

Lending (STBL) to generate bank-level estimates of small commercial loans for each year from

1980 through 1996.[6] The authors use these estimates—in tandem with Call Report data on

condition and income, structure data on consolidations and acquisitions, and Summary of

Deposits data on deposits by branch location—to quantify changes in lending attributable to

mergers and acquisitions, including supply effects attributable to nonmerging banks. Their

findings are quite dramatic. They estimate that the response of nonmerging banks generally more

than offsets the decline in small commercial loans attributable to bank consolidations. They do

not, however, specifically focus on how bank consolidation is related to small business lending in

particular types of local banking markets.

---

[5] In studies of bank branching patterns and mortgage lending patterns, Avery et al. (1999a, 1999b) find that the full
market response to consolidations can be quite different from the response of just the consolidating institutions.
Generally, Avery et al. find not only that consolidating institutions reduce their activity but also that there is virtually
always a substantial positive market offset from nonconsolidating institutions.

[6] The STBL data are reported by approximately 200 banks in a given survey wave; however, smaller independent
banks are generally not well represented in the survey (there are only about 30 at any one time). Also, the STBL,
unlike Call Reports, does not include any information about small business loans secured by commercial real estate.

Berger, Goldberg, and White (2001) study whether consolidation activity and entry by new banks can generate external effects--that is, systematic responses by other banks in the same local market.[7] They use Call Report data from 1993 to 1998 to represent a bank's small business lending and Summary of Deposits data to measure the geographic scope of the bank's markets. They relate a bank's overall small business lending to its own consolidation activity as well as to weighted measures of the consolidation activity of banks in the markets where the bank operates. Their study finds only a modest positive external effect in response to bank consolidation.

To try to address the gap in the literature regarding market-level effects, we conduct a market-level, not a bank-level, analysis. This allows us to explicitly address the behavior of institutions that are not directly involved in the local consolidation activity but that are affected by it. We are particularly interested in situations where these are community banks. We attempt to quantify the extent to which the presence (or absence) of community banks influences the impact of consolidation on small business lending at the market level both for overall lending and for various subproducts. This is the task we address in the next section.

2. METHODOLOGY AND DATA

Approximating the definitions used in antitrust analysis, we define local banking markets in terms of urban metropolitan statistical areas (MSAs) and rural counties. We study the effects of consolidation activity on changes in small business lending during two three-year study periods: 1994–1997 and 1997–2000. Related studies suggest that it takes several years for

---

[7] De novo banks tend to lend proportionately more to small businesses than mature small banks (DeYoung, Goldberg, and White, 1998); thus, they represent an interesting aspect of a market's competitive structure. Several studies have found that consolidation activity is positively related to market entry by de novo banks (Berger et al., 2000; Keeton, 2000; and Seelig and Critchfield, 2003).

consolidating institutions to restructure their behavior. For example, the integration of lending

operations, including the retraining of staff and coordination of underwriting activities, may

require considerable effort. Three years seems like a reasonable period in which to look for

consolidation-related changes in small business lending.

The core of our statistical analysis is to measure the relationship between consolidation

activity and changes in total small business lending (and in its components), testing how this

relationship is affected by the structure of the local market and the nature of the consolidation

activity. Throughout, we control for an array of banking-market characteristics and local

economic factors. Although in principle this process seems quite straightforward, in practice

there are some fairly complex issues of measurement. Here we summarize our data and

methods.[8]

Our small business loan data are from the June Call Reports.[9] As noted above, these data

do not include geographic information about where banks are lending. However, banking

institutions do report the geographic distribution of their branches and their deposits as a

_____

[8] A more detailed description of the data sources and measurement issues is presented in the data appendix to this
study.

[9] Data for commercial banks are from the Federal Financial Institutions Examination Counsel (FFEIC) Reports of
Conditions and Income (Call Reports); data for savings institutions are from the Thrift Financial Reports (TFR
Reports). Since 1993, all commercial banks and savings institutions have been required to report the number and
current outstanding balance of all commercial and agricultural loans having an original amount of less than $1
million ($500,000 for agricultural loans) in their June 30 Call Reports. Lenders report separate figures for
commercial and industrial loans not collateralized by real estate (C&I loans), loans collateralized by commercial real
estate (CRE loans), and agricultural loans. Our measure of total small business lending equals the sum of C&I and
CRE lending (and therefore excludes agricultural loans). Lenders also report total nonagricultural small business

supplement to the June Call Reports.[10] We use these geographic Summary of Deposits data for

each commercial bank or savings institution to allocate the institution's small business loans

across geographic markets, constructing midyear estimates of outstanding small business loans

for every institution in each of the markets in which it has branches. Midyear estimates of total

lending in any given market are then derived as the sum of the local lending by the institutions

operating in the market. Implicitly, our method assumes that the geographic distribution of a

bank's domestic deposits is a reasonable proxy for the geographic distribution of its small

business lending. As we summarize in the section below on robustness, related work on the

validation of data suggests that this is a reasonable assumption.

We conduct separate analyses for urban and rural markets because systematic differences

between these types of market suggest that the effects of consolidation in these markets may

differ. We exclude a number of markets from our study samples because of concerns about the

validity of results for these markets. We exclude the 20 largest MSA banking markets (defined

in terms of 1994 population), Charlotte (NC), and markets in Delaware and South Dakota

because of concerns about the dominance of large institutions and large credit card lenders in

these areas. We also exclude rural counties that in 1994 had populations below 20,000 or fewer

than four banking organizations. We estimate that the rural markets included in our study sample

account for somewhat more than two-thirds of small business lending in rural markets, while the

---

originations disaggregated into several categories based on the size of the loan commitment. Here, we differentiate
between loans with an original commitment of under $100,000 and those of a larger amount.

[10] The location (county) of banking institution depository offices and the reported deposit balances were extracted
from the annual Summary of Deposits data for commercial banks and from the Branch Office Survey System filings
for savings institutions reported in the years 1994–2000.

MSA markets we study account for just under two-thirds of small business lending in urban markets.[11]

As with any bank consolidation study, choosing a metric to quantify consolidation activity is a key step in the analysis. We define consolidation activity to include all mergers among previously unrelated banking institutions and all acquisitions by bank or thrift holding companies of previously independent institutions or holding companies.[12] Thus, our definition of consolidation activity does not include mergers among institutions that are affiliates of the same holding company. Over a three-year period, a surviving organization could have been the result of a sequence of mergers or acquisitions. We define its consolidation activity for the period as the sum of these transactions. All institutions that were unrelated at the beginning of the three-year period but are part of the same organization at the end are viewed as part of one consolidation. For a given consolidation, we define the largest of the original organizations (in terms of assets) as the acquirer and the others as the acquisitions. Local consolidation activity is defined in terms of the local institutions that were acquired; markets where no institutions were acquired are considered to have experienced no consolidation activity. Overall consolidation activity in a given market is quantified as the beginning-of-period share of the small business

---

[11] Data describing the breakdown of included and excluded markets are presented in the data appendix to this study.

[12] Transactions and structure information recorded in the Federal Reserve Board's National Information Center (NIC) database were used for these purposes.

loan market held by organizations that were acquired sometime during the subsequent 36 months.[13]

To examine how the effects of bank consolidation depend on the nature of the acquisitions taking place, we also quantify local consolidation activity in terms of two key characteristics of the parties involved in the transaction. First, we measure consolidation activity that is within market as the beginning-of-period share of the small business loan market that was acquired by organizations that also had a presence in the market before the acquisition. Second, to test if consolidation effects depend on the sizes of the institutions involved, we construct variables that decompose total consolidation activity into three components: (1) activity involving only community banks, (2) activity involving community banks being acquired by big organizations, and (3) activity involving big organizations being acquired by other big organizations. Community-bank consolidation activity in a market equals the beginning-of-period share of the small business loan market held by community banks that were subsequently acquired by other community banks during the study period. Big bank acquisitions of community banks equal the beginning-of-period share of the small business loan market funded by community banks that were subsequently acquired by big organizations. Finally, big bank acquisitions of big banks equal the beginning-of-period share of the small business loan market held by big organizations that were subsequently acquired by other big organizations.

The top segment of table 2 reports the means of the consolidation activity variables for the urban and rural samples in each study period. Urban markets are larger and less concentrated

---

[13] Our consolidation measure effectively weights an acquisition by its ex ante share of local lending in measuring its importance to the market. Thus, the acquisition of an institution that does little business lending (such as a thrift) will have only a minor impact on our measure of local consolidation activity.

than rural markets, so it is not surprising to see differences across the two groups. Urban markets experienced higher average levels of overall consolidation activity in both study periods. And not surprisingly given their larger size, urban markets tended to experience more within-market consolidation activity than did their smaller rural counterparts.[14]

In both types of markets and in both study periods, acquisitions of community banks accounted for notable shares of consolidation activity. However, rural markets are characterized by more community bank consolidation activity than urban ones, a result that—as we will document—reflects the greater presence of community banks in these smaller markets. Indeed, although overall consolidation activity was lower (on average) in rural markets, these markets experienced higher levels of community bank consolidation activity than did urban markets (on average). As noted, bank-level evidence indicates that mergers of small banks have been associated with increases in small business lending as a share of the merged entities' assets, whereas mergers involving large banks have been associated with reductions in the small business loan share of the surviving organizations. Here we test the extent to which this evidence manifests itself in terms of lending at the local market level.

Given the market-level estimates of small business lending for every bank, total lending in a given market is the sum of lending by all institutions in the market. In relating changes in small business lending to consolidation activity in a given market, we compare end-of-period

---

[14] Because most rural markets have a relatively small number of participants, consolidation activity in them was less likely to be within-market. Many rural markets experienced no consolidation activity, and in those that did, consolidation generally involved a very small number of acquisitions—often only one. Thus a particular type of consolidation activity (such as within market) was frequently the *only* type of consolidation activity in a rural market.

lending with beginning-of-period lending *net of any pro forma changes* associated with our imputation method.[15] The change in lending is expressed as a real percentage growth rate that equals the ratio of end-of-period lending to pro forma-adjusted beginning-of-period lending (both are measured in 2000 dollars). To trace consolidation-related effects on particular types of small business loans, we decompose total loan growth into *additive* components measuring (1) small business loans under $100,000 versus small business loans over $100,000, and (2) small business CRE lending versus small business C&I lending. Each of these components is expressed as a ratio, with pro forma-adjusted beginning-of-period *total* small business lending as the denominator; hence, each set of components additively equals total small business loan growth.

The middle segment of table 2 reports the means of total small business loan growth and its components for each type of market in each study period. In real terms, small business loan growth is higher (on average) in our later study period, although the growth of loans under $100,000 is lower (in fact, the mean change for these smaller loans in urban markets between 1997 and 2000 is negative). The C&I component of small business loan growth is comparable

---

[15] Because we use deposit data to estimate bank lending across markets, the merger of institutions with very different small business loan-to-deposit ratios can affect geographic loan estimates. Effectively, our method generates geographic loan estimates that reflect the overall ratio of loans to deposits of each bank and its deposits in each market. For example, if bank A and bank B lend in market j, then market j's small business loans (SBL) are calculated as SBL(j) = Deposits(a,j)(SBL (a)/Deposits(a)) + Deposits(b,j)(SBL(b)/Deposits(b)). Suppose A and B merge. If their SBL-deposit ratios differ, then SBL(j) would change if recalculated with the merged data for the two banks. More generally, if two banks have very different ratios of loans to deposits, patterns estimated using merged data for the banks would differ from patterns generated using separate data for the banks. To ensure that our market-level measures of loan growth do not reflect changes due purely to our imputation method, we calculate loan growth using (pro forma) beginning-of-period loan estimates that reflect end-of-period (post merger) organizational structures. Thus, our "adjusted" growth measures use a lending base constructed to net out any computational effects due to the combining of bank balance sheets.

(on average) in urban and rural markets and in both study periods, while the CRE component is higher for both types of markets in the 1997–2000 period. In the next section, we present tests that control for other factors to isolate patterns in these measures that are related to consolidation activity.

The bottom segment of table 2 reports the definitions and means of the control variables we include in our statistical tests. Included in our set of control variables are various measures representing the structure and competitiveness of local banking markets. One characteristic is the presence of community banks in the market, measured as the share of the local small business loan market held by community banks at the beginning of the study period. As indicated in table 2, the mean community bank market share is significantly higher in the rural samples than in the urban ones—roughly 60 percent versus 40 percent—a fact we take into consideration in our empirical tests. Our set of banking market characteristic control variables also includes a Herfendahl index of deposit market concentration, the number of organizations in the market, the share of the deposit market held by savings institutions (which tend to do proportionately less small business lending than commercial banks), and the number of banking institution branches per 10,000 residents. These variables are intended to control for the degree of competitiveness in each market at the beginning of each study period.[16] Again we find systematic differences between urban and rural markets: rural markets tend to be more concentrated and to have fewer banking organizations than urban markets.

---

[16]A Herfendahl index based on banking deposits is a standard measure used to assess the competitiveness of banking markets. The Federal Reserve Board includes thrift deposits with a weight of 50 percent in calculating Herfendahl indices for its bank merger analysis; we do the same here.

Our control variables also include several measures of market-level economic conditions. These include population, real per capita personal income, the unemployment rate, housing prices, and building permits.[17] We include levels and contemporaneous and lagged measures of change for these variables. Finally and importantly, given our method for estimating geographic lending patterns, we include both contemporaneous and lagged deposit growth in the market (as reported in the Summary of Deposits data) as control variables. Thus, we are measuring changes in small business lending attributable to consolidation activity over and above the changes associated with deposit growth in the local market.

3. STATISTICAL TESTS

Here we discuss the specific statistical tests used in our study. We begin with a discussion of the general form of the tests and follow with the results.

3.1 Tests

The basic reduced-form model that we estimate can be described by

[Small Business Loan Growth $_{(t,t+3),\,m}$] = f(Consolidation Activity$_{(t,t+3),\,m}$, Banking Market Characteristics $_{t,\,m}$, Deposit Growth$_{(t-3,t\,;\,t,t+3),\,m}$, Economic Controls$_{(t-3,t\,;\,t,t+3),\,m}$) + error,

---

[17] Data sources for the economic control variables are described in more detail in the data appendix to this study. The economic variables are constructed from annual county-level data on population and personal income (U.S. Bureau of the Census), annual county-level (establishment) data on the labor force and unemployment (U.S. Bureau of Labor Statistics), weighted-repeat-sales 1–4 family housing price indices (Fannie Mae, Freddie Mac), and annual county-level building permits (U.S. Bureau of the Census).

where t is the beginning of the three-year study period; *Small Business Loan Growth* $_{(t,t+3), m}$ equals loan growth measured (as described above) in market m from year t through year $t+3$; and *Consolidation Activity* $_{(t,t+3), m}$ measures the nature of acquisitions in market m between year t and year $t+3$. *Banking Market Characteristics* $_{t, m}$ is the set of variables measuring the characteristics of banking market m in the beginning of the study period, before the consolidation activity occurs. *Deposit Growth* $_{(t-3,t; t,t+3), m}$ and *Economic Controls* $_{(t-3,t; t,t+3), m}$ are the controls for local deposit growth and local economic conditions, respectively, during the three years before the study period (year $t-3$ through year t) and during the study period (year t through year $t+3$).

We test how the level and nature of consolidation activity and community bank presence are related to small business loan growth and its components in the following manner: First, we run regressions that include only the overall consolidation activity variable as a treatment variable. Then we run comparable regressions that replace the overall consolidation activity variable with the variables measuring the particular types of consolidation activity: (1) within-market consolidation activity, (2) big organization acquisitions of other big organizations, (3) big organization acquisitions of community banks, and (4) community bank consolidation activity. This second set of tests allows us to measure potentially differential effects of different types of consolidation activity—effects that be obscured when only the overall consolidation variable is included.

To explore the possibility that the impact of consolidation activity may differ in certain types of markets, we run two other sets of tests. First, we split each urban and rural sample on the basis of each market's degree of concentration, using the beginning-of-period Herfendahl index summarized in table 2. Markets having a beginning-of-period deposit Herfendahl index of

1800 or more are classified as *high Herfendahl* markets; all others are *low Herfendahl* markets.[18] This split allows a test of the conjecture that consolidation activity has more pronounced effects on small business credit availability in highly concentrated markets than in more competitive ones.[19] Second, we split the urban and rural samples on the basis of the prominence of community banks in the local small business loan market before the consolidation activity occurs. Rural markets where community banks have a beginning-of-period small business loan market share of 60 percent or more are classified as *high community bank share* markets; those where the community bank market share is less than 60 percent are classified as *low community bank share* markets. In the urban samples, MSAs where community banks have a beginning-of-period small business loan market share of 40 percent or more are classified as *high community bank share* markets, and those where the community bank market share is below 40 percent are classified as *low community bank share* markets. This split allows an examination of the potential mitigating impact that community banks may have on consolidation effects.

3.2 Test Results 1994–1997

   Table 3 presents results for urban markets during the 1994–1997 study period. In the interest of brevity, only coefficients for the consolidation and community bank market share variables are presented. Complete regressions are presented for a representative subset of regressions in appendix tables A.2 and A.3. Here we find a negative association between overall

---

[18] The Department of Justice's lower cutoff in its definition of highly concentrated markets is 1800.

[19] We continue to include the Herfendahl index as an explanatory variable in these tests to control for differences in concentration within the high Herfendahl and low Herfendahl subsamples.

consolidation activity and small business loan growth (panel A). This relationship is most evident in the high Herfendahl and the low community bank share subsamples. The coefficient of the community bank market share variable is positive and significant in only a few cases, and interestingly these occur in the low Herfendahl subsamples. In terms of specific types of consolidation activity (panel B), we find a consistent negative association between consolidation activity involving big organizations and small business loan growth, particularly in the high Herfendahl and low community bank share subsamples. There is some evidence of a positive effect associated with community bank consolidation activity, and again, this tends to be in the high Herfendahl and low community bank share subsamples.

Table 4 presents the results for rural markets for the 1994–1997 study period. Here we find little or no relationship between overall consolidation activity and small business loan growth, but we do find evidence of a positive effect associated with community bank market share, particularly in the low Herfendahl and the high community bank share subsamples (panel A). The only evidence of a significant overall consolidation effect is in the low community bank share subsample. The tests of specific types of consolidation activity suggest that the overall consolidation activity variable masks differential effects of different types of consolidation in rural markets during the 1994–1997 period (panel B). We find consistent evidence of a negative effect associated with consolidation activity involving big organizations and a positive effect associated with community bank consolidation activity; and again, these effects are most evident in the high Herfendahl and low community bank share subsamples. Overall, these effects appear to cancel each other out, leaving an insignificant relationship between overall consolidation activity and small business loan growth.

3.3 Test Results 1997–2000

The dynamics in small business credit markets appear to have changed in the 1997–2000 study period. Table 5 presents the results for urban markets for this period. In contrast to what we found for the 1994–1997 period, we find a positive association between overall consolidation activity and small business loan growth—a result that is evident in each of the subsamples classifying urban markets in terms of their Herfendahl index and community bank market share (panel A). These effects are evident for all subproducts but are strongest for loans under $100,000 and for C&I loans. The tests of specific types of consolidation activity (panel B) indicate that the positive overall consolidation effects are driven by consolidation activity involving big organizations. We do find negative effects associated with within-market consolidation activity in low community bank share markets, but we find no significant effects associated with community bank consolidation activity. And we find a negative association between beginning-of-period community bank market share and small business loan growth in the high Herfendahl urban subsample during the 1997–2000 period.

Table 6 presents the results for rural markets in the 1997–2000 study period. Here we find little evidence of any significant relationship between overall consolidation activity and small business loan growth (panel A). Tests of specific types of consolidation activity (panel B) indicate that big organization acquisitions of community banks are associated with higher growth in small business loans under $100,000 and in CRE lending. We find no significant effects associated with community bank consolidation activity and little evidence of a relationship between beginning-of-period community bank market share and small business loan growth in rural markets during the 1997–2000 period.

4. THE IMPACT OF CONSOLIDATION ON COMMUNITY BANKS

In the previous section, we focused on assessing the impact that the presence of community banks had on small business loan growth in markets experiencing consolidation activity. In this section, we look at a different but closely related issue—the impact of consolidation on community banks' role as small business lenders. We argued above that contractions by consolidating institutions may create opportunities for community banks as small business lenders. This can come about if existing institutions expand their lending or if new entrants come into the market. We study this issue in two ways. First, we measure changes in community bank market share for different types of small business loans in different types of markets. Then we examine the composition of small business loan growth in terms of the contributions of consolidating institutions, of existing nonconsolidating institutions, and of new market entrants. We conduct each of these investigations with data adjusted for market and economic conditions, using the same control variables as in the previous section.

Our method for examining changes in the market share of community banks as small business lenders follows. First we decompose the gross change in the share of small business loans held by community banks in a given market into three components: the pro forma change due to reclassifications in the size of organizations as a result of consolidation activity; the pro forma change due to size reclassifications resulting from asset growth (other than through acquisitions); and the change in community bank market share measured net of these pro forma changes.[20] Comparable market share change measures are constructed for each of the small

business loan components measuring CRE loans, C&I loans, loans under $100,000, and loans

over $100,000. We then regress each set of market share change measures against the set of

economic and banking market control variables used in the previous section, running separate

regressions for urban and rural markets in each of the two study periods. We include no

variables for consolidation activity in these regressions. Predictions from each set of regressions

are subtracted from their respective dependent variables to obtain gross, pro forma, and net pro

forma-adjusted community bank market share changes, all adjusted for economic and banking

market conditions. The resulting market share change variables are scaled to preserve the means

of their respective original variables.

We use a similar methodology to examine small business lending by particular types of

institutions at the local market level. First, we decompose the growth of total small business

lending and each of its subproducts into components attributable to the following groups:

consolidating institutions (within-market consolidations, out-of-market acquirers, and

acquisitions by out-of-market acquirers) differentiated by the beginning-of-period size of the

consolidated organization, existing nonconsolidating community banks, existing

nonconsolidating big organizations, community bank new market entrants, and big organization

new market entrants. The resulting set of loan growth variables are then regressed against the

---

[20] If the organization resulting from the consolidation of community banks is larger than $1 billion, the market share
of community bank lending will necessarily decrease. The pro forma variable for consolidations captures changes in
market share due purely to this effect. Similarly, when community banks have asset growth large enough to "grow
out" of the community bank classification during the measurement period, a shift in share from community banks to
large organizations is created. Yet this is not a real shift in market share because it does not represent a movement of
lending from one institution to another. The adjusted change variable reflects the change in market share netting out
both of these effects.

economic and banking market control variables, with separate regressions run for urban and rural markets in each of the two study periods. Predictions from these regressions are subtracted from their respective dependent variables and scaled to preserve the original means, yielding small business loan growth variables adjusted for economic and market factors. It should be noted that since total small business loan growth and its components are computed using the same denominator (beginning-of-period total small business lending in the market), using regressions to adjust the variables for economic and banking market factors does not change additivity: the adjusted components will still add up. Similarly, since the decompositions of loan growth into components attributable to different types of lenders use the small denominator, these components are also additive.

The results of these two procedures are presented in table 7. Values presented in the table are the sample means of the variables described above. The first eight columns report means for the 1994–1997 period and the second eight report means for the 1997–2000 period. To isolate patterns associated with consolidation activity, table 7 includes separate estimates for urban and for rural markets that are further subdivided into (1) markets experiencing no consolidation activity or a low level of it (less than 5 percent of the small business loan market was acquired), and (2) markets experiencing a high level of consolidation activity (more than 25 percent of the small business loan market was acquired). We do not report results for markets experiencing an average level of consolidation activity–that is, those where 5–25 percent of the small business loan market was acquired. Within each of these subsamples, we further classify markets in terms of whether they had a low or a high beginning-of-period community bank market share (as defined above in the section "Methodology and Data").

The top segment of table 7 presents results for changes in community bank small business loan market shares. The average community bank share of total small business lending in urban and rural markets *fell* by 1.0 and 1.3 percentage points, respectively, between 1994 and 1997, and by 2.0 and 0.5 percentage points, respectively, between 1997 and 2000 (not shown in the table). But these figures are deceptive. When pro forma changes due to size-category reclassifications (because of consolidations or asset growth) are removed, we find that on average, community bank market shares *increased* by 7.2 and 6.2 percentage points in urban and rural markets, respectively, during the 1994–1997 study period; and by 8.5 and 7.2 percentage points in urban and rural markets, respectively, during the 1997–2000 period. Thus, observed declines in community bank small business loan market shares can be attributed *entirely* to pro forma size-category reclassifications, as community banks consolidate or grow into larger organizations, rather than to any fundamental contraction in community bank lending.

The data in table 7 show fairly consistent patterns in how community bank market share changes are related to consolidation activity and beginning-of-period community bank presence. In both urban and rural markets, in both study periods, and across all types of small business loans, we find that increases in community bank market share (measured net of pro forma changes) are larger in high consolidation markets than in low consolidation markets having a similar ex ante community bank presence. We also find that the difference between net market share growth in low consolidation and high consolidation markets is greater in markets where the ex ante community bank presence is high.

These patterns suggest that the period we study was a good one for community banks as small business lenders, particularly those operating in markets undergoing consolidation. Moreover, a high ex ante community bank presence does not appear to have impeded further growth in market share; indeed, it may have enhanced such growth. Finally, we do not find

evidence supporting conjectures that large organizations were taking market share from

community banks by using standardized small business credit scoring technologies. Changes in

community bank market share measured net of pro forma effects are generally smaller for the

loans in the under $100,000 category than for larger small business loans, but in all cases their

mean change is positive.

The data in the bottom segment of table 7 provide further support for the view that the

1994–2000 period was good for community banks as small business lenders, particularly in

markets where consolidation was occurring. The growth of total small business lending

attributable to community banks ("total all CBs") is almost always higher in high consolidation

markets than in low consolidation markets having a comparable ex ante community bank

presence, even where total loan growth is lower (for example, in urban markets experiencing

high consolidation activity during the 1994–1997 period). The various decompositions of small

business loan growth indicate a broad-based pattern of growth by community banks in markets

experiencing high levels of consolidation activity. The loan growth came from all types of

community banks, including new market entrants, existing nonconsolidating institutions, and

consolidating institutions whose combined size still defined them as community banks.

During the 1994–1997 period, the greater community bank lending in high consolidation

markets contrasts with contractions by large consolidating organizations, supporting the view

that there was an "offset." However, although not shown in table 7, the data suggest that it was

in markets experiencing the acquisitions of big organizations by other big organizations where

most of the contraction in small business lending took place. During this period, we generally

find that average lending by large organizations that had acquired community banks either rose or fell only slightly in the markets where the community bank had operated. The only exceptions are markets where consolidation activity was low and ex ante community bank presence was high. In these markets, the declines in lending appear to be driven by within-market consolidations, suggesting that these areas may have been overbanked areas. Thus, it was in the consolidations of big organizations with other big organizations where significant cutbacks in small business lending occurred, creating the opportunity for community banks.

5. VALIDATION AND ROBUSTNESS

The validity of our evidence about bank consolidation and local credit availability hinges on the accuracy of the method we use to estimate the geographic distribution of small business lending. This method assumes that deposit-taking patterns are a good proxy for the geographic distribution of a bank's small business lending, both at a point in time and over time. To the extent that these patterns are dissimilar, our strategy assumes that distributional differences in lending and deposit taking are not systematically related to consolidation activity.

To assess the validity of these assumptions, we conducted two tests. First, we ran all of our statistical tests both with and without the deposit-growth control variables to examine the extent to which deposit patterns affect the results. As indicated above, deposit growth is a key factor explaining local small business loan growth—although its explanatory power varies across market subsamples. However, there is essentially no change in the estimated sign, magnitude, and significance of the key consolidation variables in the regressions estimated without the deposit variables. This indicates that our cross-market and cross-time measures of small business lending reflect more than merely variations in deposit-taking activity.

We also indirectly test the validity of our geographic loan estimates using data on small business loan originations collected under the auspices of the Community Reinvestment Act (CRA).[21] Since 1996, larger banks have been required to report the number and amount of their annual small business loan originations by census tract. Unfortunately we cannot directly replicate our study using the CRA data, since they are not reported by many of the institutions (community banks) with which we are most concerned. However, we use 1997 CRA and deposit-based small business loan measures to perform a simple comparison test for institutions that reported both types of data. Specifically, we compute the correlation of lending across markets implied by the CRA data with the distribution of loans implied by our deposit-based measures. Overall there was a .87 correlation between the two variables in the urban markets used in our study and .80 in the rural markets used, indicating a reasonable correspondence between geographic distribution of the two measures.[22]

6. CONCLUSIONS

Questions about the evolving U.S. financial environment are likely to become increasingly important as bank deregulation moves to new plateaus. Still, evidence about how factors such as bank consolidation affect the provision of traditional banking services is hard to produce. Bank

---

[21]CRA loan origination data use loan definitions comparable to those used for the small business data reported in the June Call Reports, including loan size categories and the separate reporting of agricultural and nonagricultural small business loans. Institutions representing about 70 percent of the stock of outstanding small business loans reported CRA data in 1997.

[22] More information about our comparison of geographic banking patterns evident in the Summary of Deposits and CRA data are reported in an earlier study that uses this same basic method for generating market-level small business loan estimates (Avery and Samolyk, 2000).

consolidation is inherently a complex phenomenon that affects bank customers in the particular markets for the banking services that they seek. Given the evolution of bank product markets, small business lending is likely to be one of the few products that will remain relatively local in nature.

The characterization of local consolidation activity we present in this paper yields interesting evidence about consolidation-related loan growth patterns at the local market level. In the 1994–1997 study period, we find that big organization consolidations had adverse effects on small business loan growth, whereas community bank presence and community bank merger activity were positively related to local small business credit availability. These results are broadly consistent with bank-level evidence on the effect of scale and credit culture on small business lending. The presence of community banks also appears to have mattered for local credit availability in this period, as does the competitiveness of the markets where acquisitions were taking place. We find less in the way of negative consolidation effects in markets where the ex ante community bank market share was high and market concentration was low. These findings suggest that competition in general or through a strong community bank presence can play a significant role in determining the effects of bank consolidation on the local market.

The general dynamics associated with consolidation activity in small business credit markets appear to have been quite different in the 1997–2000 study period. The relationships we do find indicate that consolidation activity involving big organizations was associated with higher local small business loan growth.

When we look at the impact of consolidation activity on community bank small business loan market shares, we find pretty consistent evidence that the 1994–2000 period in general and consolidation in particular were good for community banks. Gross market share calculations show a decline in community bank shares. But adjusted for size-category reclassifications due to consolidation or asset growth and for local market conditions, community bank small business loan market shares have increased during the 1994–2000 period. And the increases in community bank market share have been larger in markets undergoing consolidation.

Going forward, more research on small business lending at the local market level is needed to extract evidence about the role that small business lending should play in the regulation of bank consolidation. Data limitations will hamper this effort. The bank loan data we use are reported by the size of the loan rather than by the size of the borrowing firm. In addition, nonbank business lenders, such as finance companies, do not report data on their small business lending and therefore are not included in most statistical analyses of bank consolidation. Finally, researchers and policy makers must deal with issues involved in integrating the new CRA data with the other banking data traditionally used to analyze bank merger activity.

_____

DATA APPENDIX

The data used in this study combine information from sources covering three areas of commercial bank and thrift activity: (1) branch office location and deposit balances; (2) bank condition and income (including outstanding small business loans); and (3) records of bank structure (including structure changes such as failures, mergers, and acquisitions). We also use data on population, income, housing prices, employment, and building permits (issued) to measure economic conditions in local banking markets. This appendix discusses our data sources and measurement issues, including the measurement of small business loan growth and changes in community bank market share.

Data sources

The location (county) of banking institution depository offices and reported deposit balances were extracted from the annual Summary of Deposits data for commercial banks, and from the Branch Office Survey System filings for savings institutions, reported in the years 1991 through 2000. The office list includes all locations qualifying as separate institution deposit-taking offices under federal guidelines as of June 30 of each year. It does not necessarily include all drive-ins, ATMs, or loan production offices; however, virtually all staffed deposit-taking offices are reported. The geographic deposit data used in this study may differ slightly from the publicly available files as a result of limited data cleaning required for the analysis.[24]

---

[24] For example, some offices were added for a few institutions that did not submit a Summary of Deposits or Branch Office Survey System filing, and some addresses were corrected for a limited number of offices for which incorrect county location was reported. Similarly, deposit balances were imputed for some branches that reported zero

Information on outstanding small business loans was obtained from the Federal Financial Institutions Examination Counsel (FFEIC) Reports of Conditions and Income (Call Reports) and from the Thrift Financial Reports (TFR Reports) for June of each year from 1994 through 2000. Since 1993, all commercial banks and savings institutions have been required to report the number and current outstanding balance of all commercial and agricultural loans having an original amount of less than $1 million ($500,000 for agricultural loans) in their June Call Reports. Lenders report separate figures for nonagricultural small business loans not collateralized by real estate (C&I loans), loans collateralized by commercial real estate (CRE loans), agricultural loans collateralized by real estate, and other agricultural loans. Only data on C&I and CRE loans are included in our measure of small business loans. Lenders also differentiate loans by the size of the commitment. Nonagricultural loans having commitment values below and above $100,000 are differentiated in our study.

Finally, other bank-level information was needed for this study to determine the appropriate structure to use in classifying banking institutions and to determine which institutions were involved in consolidations during the study periods. Transactions and structure information recorded in the Federal Reserve Board's National Information Center (NIC) database is used for these purposes. All federally insured commercial banks and savings institutions in existence on June 30 of each year and reporting at least some small business lending are included in this study, with several exceptions. Institutions classified as wholesale, strategic-plan, or limited-purpose institutions under guidelines of the Community Reinvestment Act or as special-purpose institutions (for example, nonbank banks) by the NIC system *at any point in the 1994–2000*

---

deposits (some banks consolidate their deposits into a few offices and report zero deposit balances for the remaining offices).

period are dropped from our analysis for both study periods. Most of the excluded institutions are banks that engaged exclusively in wholesale or credit card activities. Dropped institutions are not used in computing organization sizes or in determining whether a merger or acquisition took place.

Data for most of the economic control variables were obtained from the Bureau of Economic Analysis REIS data files (annual county-level data on population and personal income), the Bureau of Labor Statistics (annual county-level [establishment] data on the labor force and unemployment), and the U.S. Bureau of the Census (county-level data on the number and dollar value of new building permits for residential homes).[25] Data on 1–4 family residential house prices are computed from the Fannie Mae and Freddie Mac weighted-repeat sales index.[26]

Variables measuring consolidation activity, small business loan growth, and economic and banking `market controls are aggregated to the market level for the analysis. All dollar-based measures used in the study—including institution size classifications—are converted to 2000 dollars using the consumer price index.

Measurement issues

This study defines markets in terms of metropolitan statistical areas (MSAs) for urban areas and in terms of counties for rural areas.[27] Hence, to construct market-level variables from

---

[25] In some cases the Census Bureau combines information for small counties or for cities in Virginia that are not included in any of the adjacent counties, and we align our data to match Census Bureau information.

[26] The index was available for a little more than one-half the MSAs, about 150 larger counties, and for states. The lowest level of aggregation possible was used to determine price changes.

[27] NECMAs (county aggregates) are used to define urban markets in New England.

county-level data, we simply aggregate data for the all counties in a given MSA. Year 2000 definitions are used to determine MSA boundaries. In all, 2,593 markets were defined, with annual information for 1994 to 2000; however, as described in this study, we exclude some markets from our study samples because of concerns about the validity of findings for very large or very small markets.[28] Overall we study 1,052 markets, including 292 MSAs and 760 rural counties.

We use the Summary of Deposits data to geographically allocate Call Report balances of outstanding small business loans as reported by a given commercial bank or savings institution across each of the markets where it operates branches. The share of an institution's total loans allocated to a given market is simply equal to the share of its total (domestic) deposits that it reports having in that MSA or county in its midyear Summary of Deposits filing. Total small business lending for a given market is therefore the sum of market-level lending estimated for each institution included in our study.

For each of the three-year periods used in our analysis, institutions are classified by their membership in banking organizations as of June 30 of the first year of the study period (1994 or

---

[28] Banking data for the largest MSAs are dominated by the behavior of the large money-center institutions concentrated in these areas. Many of these institutions have national lending programs, which may mean that our method of loan allocation is suspect. Consequently we decided to drop from the analysis the 20 largest MSAs (by deposits). Charlotte (NC) and MSAs in Delaware and South Dakota were also dropped because of the concentration of large national lending institutions in these areas. We also dropped all rural county markets that in 1994 had populations of less than 20,000 or fewer than four banking organizations having branches. These areas were felt to be too small for the impact of consolidations to be meaningfully measured. All Delaware and South Dakota rural counties were also dropped. Of the 2,593 markets in the United States, 1,522 rural counties and 25 MSAs were dropped from our analysis by the above criteria.

1997).[29] The size of an organization is computed as the sum of the domestic assets (2000

dollars) reported on the June Call Reports by all affiliated banking institutions included in our

study.[30] Commercial banks or savings institutions that are not part of a larger banking

organization are treated as independent organizations. These beginning-of-period classifications

are used to construct control variables that measure banking market structure, such as the deposit

Herfendahl indices (constructed using the Summary of Deposits data), and to classify banking

organizations as community banks (organizations having assets of less than $1 billion).

We also classify commercial banks and savings institutions in terms of these affiliations

when measuring consolidation activity occurring during a given study period. We identify the

organizational membership of each institution at the end of a given three-year study interval and

determine whether institutional affiliations changed within that interval. Institutions that were

unaffiliated at the beginning of the study period and are affiliated three years later are deemed to

have been part of a consolidation.[31]

---

[29] These organizations included bank and thrift holding companies and foreign bank payment groups (U.S. chartered
banks that are subsidiaries of a common foreign bank).

[30] This may differ somewhat from the total assets reported by bank and thrift holding companies for their combined
operations. However, consolidated information was not available for foreign bank payment groups; consequently we
decided to use a common basis in forming size. As stated above, special-purpose institutions excluded from the
study were not used in calculating organization sizes.

[31] Note that this definition of a consolidation includes mergers of previously unaffiliated institutions, acquisition of
one holding company by another, or acquisition of a previously independent institution by an existing holding
company. It does *not* include "consolidation" of common members of a bank or thrift holding company into a single
bank, as these institutions would not have been deemed to be independent at the start of the period. Note as well that
an organization acquiring a de novo bank would not be treated as having undergone a consolidation, since the de
novo institution did not exist at the beginning of the period.

For much of our analysis it is necessary to differentiate between the acquirer and the acquisition in a given consolidation. These determinations are not always apparent from the record. Consequently, we decided to designate the largest component of a consolidating entity (as measured by its size at the beginning of the period) as the acquirer. All other components were treated as acquisitions. Thus, if four previously unrelated banks merged into a common holding company within a given period, the bank with the most assets at the beginning of the period would be deemed to have acquired the other three. In characterizing different types of consolidation activity, we also classify acquirers and acquired organizations by their size. Organizations having total domestic assets of $1 billion or more (in 2000 dollars) are considered to be big; those having less are considered to be community banks.

Within a given market, a consolidation is deemed to have occurred when a bank (or organization) with small business lending in that market at the beginning of the period is acquired by another bank (or organization) during the period. For a given consolidation, if it involves a larger institution that had offices in the market before the consolidation, the consolidation is deemed to be within market; otherwise the acquisition is treated as an out-of-market consolidation. Overall consolidation activity in a market is computed as the share of the market's beginning-of-period total small business lending held by organizations that were acquired during the subsequent three-year study period. If no organization in the market was acquired, the market is deemed to have had no consolidations, and consolidation activity equals zero. Implicitly our measures of consolidation activity do not count acquisitions of institutions that report no small business lending. For example, the acquisition by a bank holding company of an independent thrift that does no small commercial lending is not counted in our measures of consolidation activity.

Table A.1: Aggregate Statistics for Subsets of Markets

	Excluded rural markets		Included rural markets		Included urban markets		Excluded urban markets	
	1994	1997	1994	1997	1994	1997	1994	1997
Population (millions)	19.4	20.0	34.1	35.1	126.3	131.2	83.4	86.3
Domestic deposits (billions of $2000)	2,050.9	2,162.4	3,972.6	4,003.0	16,089.0	16,276.9	14,170.9	14,696.8
Small business loans (billions of $2000)	283.9	328.5	576.2	622.9	1,802.1	1,930.7	1,107.6	1,226.7
Percentage of small business loans								
Held by community banks	73.6	72.6	58.1	57.2	34.9	33.5	36.3	31.2
Acquired during subsequent three years	13.9	15.1	16.2	19.0	21.8	22.2	21.4	22.1
Acquired by within-market acquirer	1.2	1.0	2.8	3.9	11.0	9.7	16.1	13.6
Mean Herfendalh index	4,656.7	4,574.4	2,262.4	2,239.4	1,627.7	1,626.4	1,364.8	1,476.7
Number of markets	1,522	1,521	760	760	292	292	25	25

Note: Statistics, except the mean Herfendahl index, are computed as aggregates for each group of markets. All variables except population are measured as of June 30 of the year. Small business lending includes C&I and commercial real estate loans that had an original denomination of less than $1 million as reported in the June 30 Call Reports and is allocated to markets using methods described in this data appendix. Community banks are organizations having beginning-of-period assets of less than $1 billion (in 2000 dollars). Acquisitions refer to the acquisitions of independent banks, savings institutions, and bank or thrift holding companies by previously unaffiliated organizations, as described in this data appendix.

Table A.1 describes the subsamples of markets that we include in our study and the markets that we exclude in terms of some of our key analysis variables. As noted in the paper, the rural markets we include in our study samples account for roughly two-thirds of small business lending in rural markets, while the MSA markets we study account for just under two-thirds of small business lending in urban markets.

Measuring small business loan growth

We measure changes in small business lending during a given three-year study period as the ratio of end-of period lending to beginning-of-period lending, with one important adjustment. Because we use the reported geographic distribution of a bank's (or thrift's) deposits to allocate its small business loans across markets, the allocation can be affected by merger activity at the bank level that changes the distribution of deposits for the merged entity. Accordingly, we calculate the beginning-of-period allocation of small business loans across markets using deposit patterns that reflect end-of-period bank-level affiliations. That is, for all banks and thrifts involved in mergers at the bank level (the level at which the Summary of Deposits and Call Report data are reported), we construct pro forma (merger-adjusted) beginning-of-period estimates of local small business lending on the basis of the geographic distribution implied by the merged entity's deposit data. These pro forma beginning-of-period small-business-loan estimates are used as the basis for measuring changes in small business lending (and in its components) over time throughout our study. The reason for this adjustment is to net out calculated changes in lending that result solely from the way bank-level mergers impact our constructed geographic loan estimates.[32]

We also decompose market-level changes in small business lending (and its components) into the parts attributable to consolidating institutions and the parts that reflect the response of other firms in the markets. Here we measure the change in lending attributable to consolidating organizations as equal to the difference between the beginning-of-period (pro forma) estimates of local lending by all consolidating parties (including acquirers) and the end-of-period lending reported by the now-consolidated organizations. Because this calculation includes the lending of acquirers, it differs somewhat from our calculation of consolidation activity in a market, which is based solely on the lending of the acquired components of the organization. Consequently, in computing loan growth attributable to consolidating institutions, we further differentiate between

---

[32] Note that holding company acquisitions do not affect our geographic loan calculations because the holding company affiliates report separate bank-level Summary of Deposits and Call Report data at both the beginning and the end of the study period; thus, the adjustment is not necessary. In contrast, although mergers of holding company affiliates are not considered consolidations by our definition, these mergers can affect the estimates of local small business lending and are therefore they are adjusted for in the computing of beginning-of-period local small business loan measures used to study changes in lending over time.

situations in which the organization had more than one component operating in the market at the beginning of the period (a within-market acquisition) and situations in which only one component operated. In the latter case, we can differentiate according to whether the market participant was the acquirer or was acquired.

In measuring the contribution of nonconsolidating institutions to market-level small business loan growth, we differentiate between institutions that operated in the market at the beginning of the period (existing institutions) and those that did not (new entrants). New entrants could be either institutions that operated in other markets at the beginning of the period and added de novo branches in the market or de novo institutions that did not operate in any market at the beginning of the period. Within the group of consolidating and nonconsolidating institutions, we further differentiate between the contributions of community banks and the contributions of large banking organizations.

Changes in community bank market share

As noted above, in studying changes in community bank small business loan market shares in local banking markets (for small business loans and each of their components: C&I loans and CRE loans, loans under $100,000, and loans over $100,000), we distinguish between pro forma changes due to reclassifications in bank size and community bank market share changes net of these pro forma changes. We measure the change in community banks' share of small business lending for a given market in a given study period in the manner that follows. For a given small business loan measure, each of the *pro forma change* components (attributable to community banks' being absorbed into larger institutions or to community banks' growing out of the $1 billion asset-size cutoff is calculated by use of the beginning-of-period pro forma market share that reclassifies the loans of community banks that will no longer be community banks by the end of the period. Note that if a community bank merger results in an institution that still has assets below the $1 billion dollar size threshold, the merger will not affect the pro forma merger calculation. The same is true for community banks that are growing but remain below the asset-size threshold at the end of the period. The pro forma change is then computed as the difference between the pro forma market share and the beginning-of-period community bank market share (technically the pro forma change could be positive if a large banking organization contracted into a community bank, but generally the pro forma change components are not positive).[33] The net change in community bank market share is thus equal to the end-of-period community bank market share less the two pro forma change components. Netting out the pro forma components due to size reclassifications allows us to examine the extent to which community banks have grown their market share—growth that is obscured if one looks only at the gross change in community bank market shares over time.

---

[33] As with the computation of our small business loan growth measures, we adjust the small business loan allocations used to compute beginning-of-period community bank market share measures to remove any possible changes due only to the merging of bank charters. Specifically, the beginning-of-period local small business lending of a bank that merges with another bank during the study period is estimated on the basis of the pro forma distribution of beginning-of-period deposits implied by the merger. The classification of this lending as community bank lending as opposed to large organization lending is then determined by the asset size of the bank's organization at the beginning of the period.

REFERENCES

Avery, R. B., R. W. Bostic, P. S. Calem, and G. B. Canner. "Consolidation and Bank Branching Patterns." *Journal of Banking and Finance* 23 (1999a), 497-532.

————. "Trends in Home Purchase Lending: Consolidation and the Community Reinvestment Act." *Federal Reserve Bulletin* 85(1999b), 81-102.

Avery, R. B., and K. A. Samolyk. "Bank Consolidation and the Provision of Banking Services: The Case of Small Commercial Loans." Working Paper 2000-01, Federal Deposit Insurance Corporation, 2000.

Berger, A. N., S. D. Bonime, L. G. Goldberg, and L. J. White. "The Dynamics of Market Entry: The Effects of Mergers and Acquisitions on De Novo Entry and Small Business Lending in the Banking Industry." Working Paper, Board of Governors of the Federal Reserve System, 2000.

Berger, A. N., R. Demsetz, and P. E. Strahan. "The Consolidation of the Financial Services Industry: Causes, Consequences, and Implications for the Future." *Journal of Banking and Finance* 23 (1999), 135-194.

Berger, A. N., L. G. Goldberg, and L. J. White. "The Effects of Dynamic Changes in Bank Competition on the Supply of Small Business Credit." *European Finance Review* 5 (2001), 115-139.

Berger, A. N., A. Saunders, J. M. Scalise, and G. F. Udell. "The Effects of Bank Mergers and Acquisitions on Small Business Lending." *Journal of Financial Economics* 50 (1998), 187-229.

Berger, A. N., and G. F. Udell. "The Economics of Small Business Finance." *Journal of Banking and Finance* 22 (1998), 613-673.

Cyrnak, A. W. "Bank Merger Policy and the New CRA Data." *Federal Reserve Bulletin* 84 (1998), 703-715.

DeYoung, R., L. G. Goldberg, and L. J. White. "De Novo Banks and Lending to Small Businesses." *Journal of Banking and Finance* 22 (1998), 463-492.

Keeton, W. R. "The Effects of Mergers on Farm and Business Lending at Small Banks: New Evidence from Tenth District States." Working Paper, Federal Reserve Bank of Kansas City, 1997.

————. "Are Mergers Responsible for the Surge in New Bank Charters?" Federal Reserve Bank of Kansas City *Economic Review,* Quarter 1 (2000), 21-41.

Morgan, D. P., and K. A. Samolyk. "Geographic Diversification in Banking: Implications for Bank Portfolios and Performance." Working Paper, Federal Deposit Insurance Corporation, 2003 (forthcoming).

Peek, J., and E. S. Rosengren. "Bank Consolidation and Small Business Lending: It's Not Just Size That Matters." *Journal of Banking and Finance* 22 (1998), 799-819.

Samolyk, K. A. "Small Business Credit Markets: Why Do We Know So Little About Them?" *FDIC Banking Review* 10:2 (1997), 14-32.

Samolyk, K. A., and C. Richardson. "Bank Consolidation and Small Business Lending within Local Banking Markets." Working Paper 2003-02, Federal Deposit Insurance Corporation, 2003.

Seelig, S. A., and T. Critchfield. "Determinants of De Novo Entry in Banking." Working Paper 2003-01, Federal Deposit Insurance Corporation, 2003.

Strahan, P. E., and J. Weston. "Small Business Lending and the Changing Structure of the Banking Industry. *Journal of Banking and Finance* 22 (1998), 821-845.

Whalen, G. "Out-of-State Holding Company Affiliations and Small Business Lending." Economic and Policy Analysis Working Paper 95-4, Office of the Comptroller of the Currency, 1995.

Table A.3: Effects of Overall Consolidation Activity (CA) and Local Community Bank (CB) Market Share on Small Business Loan Growth: 1997-2000

Effects on small business loan (SBL) growth and its decompositions into loans under and over $100,000 and CRE versus C&I loans. Estimated coefficients and standard errors (reported in parentheses) for all explanatory variables

	Urban Markets					Rural Markets				
	Total SBL	<$100K SBL	>$100K SBL	CRE SBL	C&I SBL	Total SBL	<$100K SBL	>$100K SBL	CRE SBL	C&I SBL
Intercept	29.961 ***	2.778	27.182 ***	16.456 ***	13.504 *	55.449 ***	29.772 ***	25.676 ***	35.310 ***	20.138 ***
	(10.34)	(7.050)	(7.761)	(5.827)	(8.009)	(10.38)	(8.384)	(8.938)	(7.666)	(5.483)
Overall CA	0.102 *	0.084 **	0.018	0.002	0.100 **	0.021	0.057 *	-0.036	0.016	0.005
	(0.052)	(0.036)	(0.039)	(0.030)	(0.041)	(0.042)	(0.034)	(0.036)	(0.031)	(0.022)
CB SBL mkt share	-0.016	-0.025	0.009	-0.015	0.000	-0.003	-0.047 *	0.044	-0.005	0.002
	(0.046)	(0.032)	(0.035)	(0.026)	(0.036)	(0.032)	(0.026)	(0.028)	(0.024)	(0.017)
Number of banks	0.104	0.069	0.035	0.019	0.085	-0.133	0.023	-0.155	-0.332	0.199
	(0.120)	(0.082)	(0.090)	(0.068)	(0.093)	(0.487)	(0.393)	(0.419)	(0.360)	(0.257)
Deposit Herfendahl	0.002	0.001	0.001	0.000	0.003 *	-0.006 ***	-0.004 ***	-0.003 *	-0.005 ***	-0.002 **
	(0.002)	(0.001)	(0.001)	(0.001)	(0.002)	(0.002)	(0.001)	(0.001)	(0.001)	(0.001)
Offices per-capita	-0.559	0.377	-0.936	0.312	-0.871	1.238	0.460	0.778	0.828	0.410
	(1.575)	(1.074)	(1.182)	(0.888)	(1.220)	(0.856)	(0.691)	(0.737)	(0.632)	(0.452)
Deposits per-capita	-4.389	-1.776	-2.613	-3.963	-0.425	-25.47 ***	-12.20 ***	-13.28 ***	-14.73 ***	-10.75 ***
	(4.337)	(2.957)	(3.255)	(2.444)	(3.359)	(3.170)	(2.560)	(2.729)	(2.341)	(1.674)
Deposit growth lagged	-0.002	-0.059	0.056	0.028	-0.030	0.092	0.180 *	-0.088	0.091	0.001
	(0.062)	(0.042)	(0.047)	(0.035)	(0.048)	(0.114)	(0.092)	(0.098)	(0.084)	(0.060)
Deposit growth current	0.785 ***	0.343 ***	0.442 ***	0.174 ***	0.611 ***	1.199 ***	0.593 ***	0.605 ***	0.748 ***	0.451 ***
	(0.061)	(0.042)	(0.046)	(0.035)	(0.048)	(0.056)	(0.045)	(0.048)	(0.042)	(0.030)
Thrift deposit share	0.033	0.005	0.029	-0.009	0.042	0.021	0.004	0.017	0.002	0.019
	(0.087)	(0.059)	(0.065)	(0.049)	(0.067)	(0.063)	(0.051)	(0.054)	(0.047)	(0.033)
Population lagged	-0.052	-0.008	-0.044	-0.028	-0.024	-1.293 ***	-1.085 ***	-0.207	-0.690 *	-0.603 **
	(0.038)	(0.026)	(0.028)	(0.021)	(0.029)	(0.493)	(0.398)	(0.425)	(0.364)	(0.261)
Pop. growth lagged	-0.037	-0.075	0.039	0.489	-0.526	0.239	-0.186	0.424	0.255	-0.016
	(0.632)	(0.431)	(0.474)	(0.356)	(0.489)	(0.373)	(0.302)	(0.321)	(0.276)	(0.197)
Pop. growth current	0.728	0.238	0.490	0.266	0.462	-0.515	-0.322	-0.192	-0.096	-0.419 *
	(0.710)	(0.484)	(0.533)	(0.400)	(0.550)	(0.446)	(0.360)	(0.384)	(0.330)	(0.236)
Per-cap income lagged	-6.257 *	-1.842	-4.415 *	-1.918	-4.339 *	6.467 *	1.913	4.554	4.398 *	2.069
	(3.337)	(2.275)	(2.504)	(1.880)	(2.584)	(3.470)	(2.802)	(2.987)	(2.562)	(1.833)
PC income growth lagged	0.452	0.302	0.150	0.020	0.432 *	0.151	-0.091	0.242	-0.027	0.177
	(0.321)	(0.219)	(0.241)	(0.181)	(0.249)	(0.241)	(0.194)	(0.207)	(0.178)	(0.127)
PC income growth current	0.231	-0.008	0.239	-0.059	0.290	0.331	0.117	0.214	0.176	0.156
	(0.317)	(0.216)	(0.238)	(0.179)	(0.246)	(0.269)	(0.218)	(0.232)	(0.199)	(0.142)
UE rate lagged	-0.443	-0.244	-0.199	-0.175	-0.268	-0.603	-0.128	-0.475	-0.239	-0.364 *
	(0.414)	(0.283)	(0.311)	(0.234)	(0.321)	(0.414)	(0.334)	(0.356)	(0.306)	(0.219)
UE rate change lagged	1.633 *	0.386	1.247 *	0.795	0.838	-0.022	-0.549	0.528	-0.461	0.440
	(0.898)	(0.613)	(0.674)	(0.506)	(0.696)	(0.533)	(0.431)	(0.459)	(0.394)	(0.282)
UE rate change current	1.749 *	0.890	0.859	0.579	1.171	0.277	0.360	-0.082	0.562	-0.284
	(1.015)	(0.692)	(0.762)	(0.572)	(0.786)	(0.606)	(0.490)	(0.522)	(0.448)	(0.320)
House price index chg lagged	0.125	-0.158	0.283 **	0.106	0.019	0.154	-0.168	0.322 **	0.075	0.079
	(0.157)	(0.107)	(0.118)	(0.089)	(0.122)	(0.157)	(0.126)	(0.135)	(0.116)	(0.083)
House price index chg current	-0.004	0.022	-0.026	0.097	-0.101	-0.391 **	-0.200	-0.191	-0.249 *	-0.142
	(0.155)	(0.105)	(0.116)	(0.087)	(0.120)	(0.174)	(0.140)	(0.150)	(0.128)	(0.092)
Bldg permits % chg lagged	-0.002	-0.009	0.007	0.016	-0.018	-0.056 *	-0.019	-0.037	-0.051 **	-0.005
	(0.048)	(0.033)	(0.036)	(0.027)	(0.037)	(0.032)	(0.026)	(0.027)	(0.023)	(0.017)
Bldg permits % chg current	-0.106 **	-0.046	-0.060 *	-0.037	-0.068 *	-0.036	-0.042	0.007	-0.038	0.002
	(0.045)	(0.031)	(0.034)	(0.025)	(0.035)	(0.032)	(0.026)	(0.028)	(0.024)	(0.017)
R-Square	0.486	0.272	0.414	0.302	0.440	0.432	0.226	0.231	0.366	0.272
Sample size	292	292	292	292	292	760	760	760	760	760
Dependent variable mean	16.344	-0.573	16.918	8.944	7.401	18.980	0.220	18.760	12.040	6.937

Note: *, **, *** indicate significance levels of 10%, 5%, and 1%, respectively.